Mindful Relationship Habits

THE 12 MOST IMPORTANT PRACTICES
FOR COUPLES TO ENHANCE INTIMACY,
NURTURE CLOSENESS, AND GROW A
DEEPER CONNECTION

© Copyright 2020 - All Rights Reserved.

The content contained within this book may not be reproduced, duplicated or transmitted without direct written permission from the author or the publisher.

Under no circumstances will any blame or legal responsibility be held against the publisher, or author, for any damages, reparation, or monetary loss due to the information contained within this book. Either directly or indirectly.

Legal notice:

This book is copyright protected. This book is only for personal use. You cannot amend, distribute, sell, use, quote or paraphrase any part, or the content within this book, without the consent of the author or publisher.

Disclaimer notice:

Please note the information contained within this document is for educational and entertainment purposes only. All effort has been executed to present accurate, up to date, and reliable, complete information. No warranties of any kind are declared or implied. Readers acknowledge that the author is not engaging in the rendering of legal, financial, medical or professional advice. The content within this book has been derived from various sources. Please consult a licensed professional before attempting any techniques outlined in this book.

By reading this document, the reader agrees that under no circumstances is the author responsible for any losses, direct or indirect, which are incurred as a result of the use of information contained within this document, including, but not limited to, errors, omissions, or inaccuracies.

TABLE OF CONTENTS

CHAPTER 1: BENEFITS OF BUILDING A MINDFUL RELATIONSHIP 8
- Importance of Relationships 8
- Personality and Social Development 10

CHAPTER 2: HOW TO BUILD A MINDFUL RELATIONSHIP HABITS? 14
- Eight Habits to Cultivate 16
- Practice Loving Kindness 16
- Own Your Feelings with "I" Statements 17
- Find Out What Makes Your Partner Feel Loved 18
- Practice daily Acts of Love 19
- Tell Your Partner What You Need 20
- Take Care of Yourself 21
- Disconnect from Digital Devices 21
- Be Open to Vulnerability 23

CHAPTER 3: PRIORITIZE YOUR RELATIONSHIP WITH MEETINGS 24
- How Do You Grow this Habit? 25
- Discuss a Day and a Time of Day that Fits Well for Both of You 25
- Set Up a Series of Reminders or Prompts for a Meeting 25
- Please Take Notes in the Journal during the Conference 26
- Set the Mood of the Conference 26
- Have a Meeting Agenda 27
- Please Mind Your Job for the Coming Week 28

CHAPTER 4: LEAD WITH RESPECT AND KINDNESS .. 30

CHAPTER 5: CHERISH YOUR PARTNER 36

TAKING CHARGE OF YOUR EMOTIONS ON YOUR RELATIONSHIP 37
STRATEGIES FOR TRUSTING ON YOUR PARTNER 40
TRUST-BUILDING EXERCISES 40
FALL BACK 41

CHAPTER 6: TOUCH OFTEN 42

CHAPTER 7: CREATE SHARED RITUALS 46

WHY IS TROUBLE BEING FUN-LOVING? 46
WHAT DOES ROMANTIC PLAY RESEMBLE? 47
WHAT SORT OF PLAY WILL WORK FOR YOU? 49

CHAPTER 8: DEVELOP ACTIVE LISTENING 52

LEARN ACTIVE LISTENING 55

CHAPTER 9: MANAGE YOUR ANGER 58

UNDERSTANDING THE IMPACT OF ANGER ON YOUR RELATIONSHIP 59
HOW WE GET ENTANGLED 60
WHAT OPTIONS DO YOU HAVE? 60
THE NATURE OF CHANGE IN RELATIONSHIPS 61
LEARNING A NEW PATTERN 62

CHAPTER 10: REDUCE THE USE OF SOCIAL MEDIA AND DIGITAL DEVICES 64

CHAPTER 11: LEARN TO LOVE YOURSELF 70

WHY IS IT SO IMPORTANT TO LOVE YOURSELF? 71
FACTS ABOUT SELF LOVE IN RELATIONSHIPS 71
HOW TO LOVE YOURSELF? 74

CHAPTER 12: APOLOGIZE MORE OFTEN 78

ADMIT YOUR MISTAKES 79
LEARN TO RESPECT, THE EMOTIONS OF YOUR PARTNER 80
BE SINCERE WITH YOUR APOLOGY 80

Humble Yourself and Ask for Forgiveness 81
Forgive Yourself 82
Create an Action Plan 82
Put Your Action Plan into Practice 83

CHAPTER 13: SPICE UP YOUR SEX LIFE 84

Dirty Weekend Getaway 87
Play a Game 88
Talk about Your Fantasies 88
Switch Things Up 89
New Lingerie 89
Be a little naughty 90
Double the Foreplay 90
Daytime Flirting! 91
Shush the Bedroom Ambiance 91
Add Sex Slots to the Calendar 92

CHAPTER 14: PRACTICE EMPATHY 94

Acknowledge Your Partner's Pain 94
Share Your Feelings 95
Show Your Partner that You Are Grateful When They Open Up to You 95
Show Your Partner that You Are Interested 96
Show Encouragement 97
Show Support 98

CONCLUSION 100

CHAPTER 1:

Benefits of Building a Mindful Relationship

Importance of Relationships

There is ample evidence that correlations, often substantial, exist between quality and quantity of relationships and diverse outcomes, including mortality rates, coronary artery bypass surgery, immune system functioning, stress reactions, mental disorder, and life satisfaction.

How have the mechanisms developed through which relationship events influence human biology? Some sources suggest that living and working in small, cooperative communities was the primary survival strategy for the human species since early humans were buffered by the social organizations from the dangers of nature.

Individuals are mainly psychologically attached to careers and intimates, and collaboration predominates among in-groups. Social interaction requires deciding what kind of relationship occurs, and hence the essential processes.

Relationships can be described in terms of the properties that define the parties' interdependence involved with how individuals change their conduct to comply with others' behaviors and desires. Therefore, persons in relationships respond (or not) to each other's desires, interests, skills, and emotional expressions; change their actions to be together (or not); delegate tasks to one another; react to each other's activities and circumstances, misery, and happiness; and take into account the fact of their interdependence in the organization of daily and long-term existence The belief that such patterns of reciprocal interaction are more insightful about relationships than abstract categories (e.g., partners, employers, friends) or basic static descriptors (e.g., length of association, existence or degree of effect) is fundamental to most conceptualizations of relationships. There is evidence of differential effects of the relationship contexts in many research areas. We then identify such areas to explain the importance of the psychological science of such evidence.

Personality and Social Development

Most personality development theories argue that maturity and aging are cognitive transition times, discontinuity, and earlier life habits transformation. It is assumed that these changes occur concerning the demands of the increasing biological status and social context of the person — the family, the workplace, and society in general. Thus, the development of personality is both a unique phenomenon and a social one.

For example, the young adult is expected to enter an institution that is, marriage and family — that will reinforce the community.

In such a relationship, the degree to which the essential need for intimacy at all levels physical, emotional, and others is fulfilled defines in most individuals the conception of the self as belonging or as alienated. The problem arises between the sense of generativity and the sensation of stagnation in middle adulthood. The person is expected to play the role of a participating, generative member of society at this point. Generativity may take the form of delivering the goods and services through which society functions or creates, rearing, and socializes future members of society. A sense of depression stems from the inability to develop a positive self-conception. According to Erikson, in adulthood, a conflict occurs over ego dignity versus the sense of desperation. At this stage, people realize they're reaching the end of life. If they have advanced successfully through the preceding stages of development, they will face old age with comfort in the feeling that they have led a complete life. Individuals lacking this quality in life frequently feel a sense of desperation for "wasted" opportunities.

During this time, critical life events include job choice, first work, marriage, and childbirth. The age range from 28 to 33 years reflects a transition from adult entry to the following settling period. The transition provides an opportunity for the young man to adapt and enrich the adult life's provisional framework that he created earlier. However, a moderate to a severe crisis is typical for most men; divorce and job changes are widespread during this period. There follows a settling-down period, starting in the early 30s and lasting until about age 40. During this time, the man's task is to become a full-fledged adult, underlines stability, and health. The individual makes deeper commitments to their profession, family, or whatever business is crucial to him. However, he also concentrates on "making it." This includes long-range preparation with a timeline for their achievement against specific goals. Many people focus on a critical event in life, such as promotion, as a symbol of society's ultimate affirmation.

The change to midlife lasts four to six years, peaking in the early 40s. This establishes a generational link between early adulthood and middle adulthood and reflects a beginning and end, a convergence of past and future, being part of both ages. A midlife change goal focuses on this gap between what is and what could be partly resolved. The transition may be relatively smooth, but significant instability is more likely to occur. The initiation period of middle adulthood starts at about age 45 and lasts to around age 50. Sometimes, the beginning of this new life structure is marked by a significant event in life, such as a change of job or occupation or a divorce or love affair. In other instances, the modifications are subtler.

Similarly, age-related traits are based on the socio-adaptation facets of personality, e.g., goal-driven behavior, coping styles, and life satisfaction. Consequently, it seems that how healthy adults communicate with the world can be constant, even though their roles shift with age. On the other hand, it revealed marked age differences in individual styles of dealing with the inner world of experience. For instance, 40-year-olds felt responsible for their environment, viewed the self as a source of energy, and were optimistic about risk-taking. Simultaneously, 60-year-olds saw the environment as challenging and even dangerous and viewed the self as passive and welcoming.

CHAPTER 2:

How to Build a Mindful Relationship Habits?

One primary goal of mindfulness practice is to develop the ability to shift your perspective from narrow to complete.

This means refocusing from the small picture (daily chores, daily irritations, closed-off emotions, or narrow views) to the big picture (deep connections with other people, your role in the world, emotional openness, or broad views).

When we operate from a narrow perspective, we feel fearful and defensive, closed-off to anything that might hurt us.

When we operate from a broad perspective, we feel calm and free, open to anything that life may bring.

Narrow Perspective	Broad Perspective
Daily tasks	Life goals
Irritations and resentments	Deep connections with others
Getting through the day	A sense of purpose
Needy	Centered
Anxious	Calm
Emotionally closed	Emotionally open
Self-centered	Part of a greater whole

Of course, there is a time and a place for both perspectives. No one can live in the big picture all the time. Even monks have to wash the dishes. That's how mindfulness practices were developed in the first place. When Buddhist monks had to take a break from meditation to do necessary chores, they tried to stay in the meditative mindset by focusing intently on what they were doing. It might seem like a paradox, but just paying attention to the present moment is often all it takes to switch your perspective to the big picture.

Eight Habits to Cultivate

Here are some mindful relationship habits you can start cultivating right away:

1. Practice, loving-kindness.

2. Own your feelings with "I" statements.

3. Find out what makes your partner feel loved.

4. Practice daily acts of love.

5. Tell your partner what you need.

6. Take care of yourself.

7. Disconnect from digital devices.

8. Be open to vulnerability.

Practice Loving Kindness

The mindful way to begin any conversation is with loving-kindness. This doesn't mean you can never raise any issues with your partner or that you must avoid conflict at all costs.

Loving-kindness isn't fake and doesn't require you to suppress your real emotions behind a plastered-on smile.

Own Your Feelings with "I" Statements

You may have heard about the benefits of using "I" statements rather than "you" statements. Even if you've heard it all before, the benefits are real. "I" statements take ownership over your feelings rather than projecting them onto your partner. They are much less likely to make your partner feel criticized or attacked, so they are much less likely to trigger an adverse reaction.

Using "I" statements instead of "you" statements is mindful and a form of mindfulness training in its own right. To develop the habit of using "I" statements, you'll have to slow down and think about everything you say to your partner before you say it. The act of slowing down and paying close attention is the basis of every mindfulness exercise, so you can improve your ability to be mindful just by making a conscious effort to develop this habit.

Find Out What Makes Your Partner Feel Loved

People don't all express love in the same way because people don't all want to receive love in the same way.

When both partners are giving the type of love they yearn to receive, they'll both feel unloved unless they happen to yearn for the same thing.

It's like they're speaking different languages.

According to Marriage Counselor Gary Chapman, most People Fit into one of five "Love Languages":

- **Words:** The use of loving words such as compliments, supportive statements, or romantic expressions.

- **Time:** Spending time fully engaged with each other without distractions of any kind. This can be as simple as playing a board game together or going for a walk, as long as your attention is entirely on your partner.

- **Presents:** Giving and receiving gifts such as jewelry, flowers, chocolate, journals — anything the other person will enjoy receiving

- **Service:** Doing things for the other person, like getting a glass of water or running an errand

- **Touch:** This can be anything from a hug to sexual intimacy. Some people are more focused on cuddling and physical closeness, and some are more focused on sexual touch, but either way, the physical connection is central.

The easiest way to find out what makes your partner feel loved is just to ask, but if your communication has broken down, this may not be so easy. If your partner isn't in touch with their feelings, they might not even be able to articulate what they need.

Practice daily Acts of Love

Once you know which love language your partner responds to. You can work that language into your daily life. For example, you could set aside a little time every day to give your partner your undivided personal attention, or you could take one errand or chore off their hands every day. You could make a point of coming home with flowers or other little gifts. You could make sure to hug them often and warmly.

Tell Your Partner What You Need

Expecting other people to be mind-readers is rarely effective and usually results in bitterness and resentment on both sides. Remember, your partner is probably trying to tell you how they feel even if you can't hear them — it's just that they're speaking in their love language rather than yours.

For example, perhaps you feel unloved because your partner is always giving you gifts you don't even want but never gets you a glass of water or carries something massive for you. Your partner is trying to speak the language of gifts when the language you understand best is service acts. Remember to talk about your feelings, not their actions. "I love being held and need more cuddle time" has a good chance of being heard, but "you never want to cuddle with me" does not.

Take Care of Yourself

When you rely on your partner to provide everything you need in life, you put far too much weight on the relationship, and it inevitably suffers under strain. Of course, you want your partner to add something extraordinary to your life that wouldn't otherwise be there, but that doesn't mean they can meet every unresolved need you've ever had. No one can make you "feel whole" if you don't feel whole already.

Disconnect from Digital Devices

Everyone knows that digital devices are convenient, entertaining — and frequently distracting. If they weren't so good at claiming your attention, you wouldn't use them in the first place. Unfortunately, these devices have become so effective at claiming our attention that they alienate us from the people we love the most.

One of the best things you can do for your relationship is to give it your full attention and emotional engagement whenever possible.

This means disconnecting from digital devices when you're spending time together. Many people find it helpful to try to follow these rules:

- No device is used when you're having dinner together.
- No device is used when you're on a date together.
- Scheduled "no device" time whenever you both have the day off. You may not be able to shut the device off all day, but you should schedule as much device-free time as possible.
- Do things outside like going for a walk together, and don't bring your devices with you.
- Whenever possible, talk in person rather than send text messages.

Digital devices continually pull you away from the present moment. Every time you hear the alert and check your smartphone to see who texted you, your attention is drawn away from whatever you're doing at that moment. Digital devices always encourage you not to be mindful, and disconnecting from them will make it much easier to stay focused on your relationship.

Be Open to Vulnerability

This means two things at once: be open to your partner's vulnerability, and be open to your own. Vulnerability and intimacy go hand in hand. If you don't trust someone enough to show them who you are, how close are you ever likely to be? Vulnerability feels dangerous because someone who knows your inner weaknesses can take advantage of that information and do you serious harm. That's why it isn't usually a good idea to jump into an intimate relationship too quickly. Sharing vulnerabilities or asking you to do so too quickly is a red flag. Someone who does this might be a potential abuser trying to get a hook into you.

CHAPTER 3:

Prioritize Your Relationship with Meetings

Most of us would say we put our relationship first, but do we do that? Do we frequently offer priority to our relationship and our spouse or partner before jobs, digital devices, personal interests, and others?

Are we willing to sacrifice our time, resources, and emotional comfort to make sure we don't risk the intimacy, confidence, respect, and affection we share with our partner?

This is not a meeting to discuss your children, your lists of tasks, or your upcoming holiday. It's just a meeting to reflect on your relationship and discuss ways to make it stronger and healthier, and it should be the first habit that you set up together.

How Do You Grow this Habit?

If you're going through a severe struggle or dispute, you can meet every day until you feel like things are back on track and you've resolved. Otherwise, try to meet once a week or twice a month.

Discuss a Day and a Time of Day that Fits well for both of You

Choose a time when infants, jobs, or other life demands are less likely to be disrupted. Often, think of a moment when you're not under stress or pressure. It's probably not a good time until you leave for work in the morning. It would be easier to have a Sunday morning or an evening after the children are in bed.

Set Up a Series of Reminders or Prompts for a Meeting

This is particularly relevant if you only meet once a week or twice a week. The only tool that Steve suggests is Google Calendar. He and his wife use this method to share their schedule, including meetings, appointments, and upcoming activities related to their son. This makes it relatively easy for both of them to know precisely what the other person is doing at any point in the day. Only focus on your one habit for the first week to get the hang of it. Your following meeting to review your progress might not take too long, but you will appreciate your efforts' early success.

Please Take Notes in the Journal during the Conference

Both of you should take notes during your meetings to keep track of your success. This helps you see how your relationship and intimacy are changing and see what you need to continue working on. During the meetings, you should write down suggestions, questions, or issues that you would like to discuss at the following meeting.

Set the Mood of the Conference

Try not to participate in debates or uncomfortable conversations before the conference, but not add negative energy. If you are too upset to have a constructive conversation, postpone your meeting until you are calmer.

Choose a meeting place conducive to a private, fruitful, respectful dialogue in which all partners feel equal. Delete any obstacles, such as computers and phones. Make sure that everyone else in the house knows not to disturb you.

Have a Meeting Agenda

Your discussions would be much more efficient if you decide what you want to do — whether separately or on both sides.

If you're working on a new habit of strengthening your relationship, explore this habit after talking about good things.

Take turns expressing how well you think you've done with this new behavior and how well you think your partner has done.

Neither of you must attempt to mitigate your partner's feelings by justifying or deflecting your actions or denying that your partner's feelings are justified. Your joking remark may have been innocent, but your partner's feelings should be your priority.

Please Mind Your Job for the Coming Week

Based on what you mentioned at the meeting and the work you both need to do; discuss the steps you plan to take throughout the week to progress. Write it down in your diaries to remember the following week. Then end the meeting the same way you started it — with a hug, a kiss, and words of affirmation.

CHAPTER 4:

Lead with Respect and Kindness

Being kind is one of the best things you can do to mend your relationship. When you aren't getting along with your partner, passions are flying in the wrong way. Both of you want to be right, want to state your points. A lot of kindness can be lost in these moments because you likely feel frustrated and exhausted by the relationship's dynamic. All couples' fight; it is inevitable. What matters is how you are communicating during your disagreements and what you do after they are over. Those who continually "make up" without making any changes will only find themselves in the same situation again in the future.

If you know that you are in a bad mood or angry with your partner, do not jump into an in-depth discussion. You need to take some time for yourself to calm down and collect your thoughts. The things you say out of anger are often the most regrettable, so your aim should be to avoid this at all costs. If something is becoming too much for you, ask for a little alone time to gather yourself. Take some deep breaths to empty your mind and find your center. Once you feel that you are calming down, get to the root of your facing. Figure out what is causing you to feel gloomy and why. You won't always have clear answers, but calming yourself down before you talk to your partner will automatically result in a better outlook for the two of you.

Couples need hobbies of their own, space to exist outside of the relationship. When you spend too much time together, there is a higher chance you will become frustrated with one another. This is when kindness is forgotten. If you just feel that you cannot get along, you might need to spend some time doing things that you individually enjoy. Plus, distance makes the heart grow fonder. When you are away from your partner, either hanging out with friends or engaging in a personal hobby, you will begin to miss certain aspects of being with them. Taking some time to do activities apart does not mean your relationship has to suffer. It can be one of the healthiest decisions you make as a couple.

Your partner is the closest person to you. Because you know each other so well, you also know that the love you have for each other is unconditional. For this reason, it becomes easy to take your anger out on your partner subconsciously. Even if they haven't done anything wrong, projecting your frustrations onto them might feel okay because you know they will forgive you. This doesn't mean it is fair, though. When you are feeling down, make sure you take full accountability for why this is happening. Do not place this burden on your partner. If you need to talk about the issue, you can vent to your partner, but do not misdirect any of your anger toward them. This will only create a combative situation where kindness will go out the window.

In any situation, you can likely feel when things are getting tense. If the tension rises too much, you will slip up and say something you don't mean. Part of anger management is avoiding these situations before they blow up. If you are in a heated discussion with your partner, you cannot calm down and vocalize that you need some time to think. If they do the same to you, respect their wishes. This will allow the situation to settle down and give you both the chance to think before you speak. So many people who run their mouths end up feeling regret and guilt once everything has been said. You don't want to be left with these feelings.

Think about why you first started dating your partner, what you love most about them. Getting back to your roots can bring up a renewed feeling of kindness. Do some of the things that you used to do for them before you two were official. These courting gestures usually disappear once you make things official, but they do not have to. The same goes for flirting — continue to flirt with your partner, even if you have been together for a while! It is very kind of you to think about your partner's enjoyment and how you can bring more of this into their life. Try to do nice things for them always, not just on special occasions. Your actions will speak volumes.

Kindness also builds trust. If your partner knows that you can respond kindly to anything, they will feel safe telling you everything. Those with explosive tempers often push their partners away or become abusive because they cannot get over their own internalized insecurities. Being open-minded and kind is the way to go. You should want your partner to feel comfortable telling you anything, even if it is unpleasant. That is the beauty of honesty and healthy communication. If your temper has been wrong in the past, it is not too late to change this. Make bold choices that will show your partner that you want them to feel safe and comfortable.

CHAPTER 5:

Cherish Your Partner

If they repeat the mistake or do something similar, then your understanding and hope begin to head from the window. After that, your partner is frequently reminded of the inability to keep their word, and they're judged according to what happened. The relationship changes and the guilty partner might find him/herself reluctant to invest in it, as the outcomes aren't always positive.

When you stop allowing your partner to redeem themselves, then you've undoubtedly also stopped believing in him/her.

Whatever they may tell you, a little voice in your head will start reminding you that you should not trust them. Then, before you realize what happened, there will be frustration, discord, and pain in your relationship.

That's the point where you start to become suspicious, and your ideas can negatively influence your activities. Sometimes you might believe that your partner did something, even if you've got zero proof to back up your idea; many of the things they say seem to be a lie.

Jealousy stems from a lack of confidence and fear, and it induces insecurity and nervousness in the relationship. Whenever you're jealous, insecure, and nervous, you're permanently on the watch for unproven lies or inconsistencies out of your partner. You patiently wait for them to slide up, proving that your concerns were set. Your feelings are rooted in fear, and even though you attempt to find proof to back up your ideas, you do it with your heart continuously racing because of hope.

Taking Charge of Your Emotions on Your Relationship

The very first step to take care of your jealousy is to understand and admit that you're doubtful of your partner. Being aware of it will block you from blaming them for your feelings and helping them do something to solve the issue. Once you admit your emotions, you enable yourself to fix your relationship. From the moment you understand that you're making a conscious choice in being jealous, you can discharge that anxiety and opt to trust your loved one.

You may start by looking at your partner with a new pair of eyes, looking at what he/she does with a positive and proactive attitude, instead of a cynical and negative one. This suggestion isn't quite as simple as it might sound, but it may be accomplished.

This usually means that you decide to leave the past in the past and 'judge' your partner's actions starting today. It's hard, but living the present can be quite liberating; not having any negative feelings or background concerns lets you trust your partner better when telling you something.

You won't prejudge their behavior, and you won't wind up unhappy painful memories. When your partner calls to let you know they'll be working late, assure him/her that it's okay and hang up the telephone; don't start asking a lot of questions like where are you? Who are you with? What are you doing? Why are you doing that to me?

Instead, you might ask questions like if they're okay, have they had something to eat, or would they enjoy a hot bath when they get home.

This attitude will probably not place your partner in a defensive mood; actually, he/she might start rushing to complete everything sooner, so they could come home to a loving setting. After the telephone call, rather than sitting and imagining your partner with another individual, envision them doing exactly what they told you they were about to do. So, when they get home, they're most likely to come across a more relaxed you, seeking to help them get a load of stress off their shoulders.

Keep in mind that if they break your confidence and they lie to you, they are not making a fool out of you. They are making a fool out of themselves. In cases like this, they're the ones harming the relationship, and you'd be justified in choosing to leave.

You aren't accountable for their behavior. You're only for your own, such as the way you respond to the situations. Trust is the basis of any relationship.

Strategies for Trusting on Your Partner

What both of you have to do is to find out how to trust each other. One of the best ways to start doing it is to believe on your own. In reality, trusting yourself is the first thing that anyone must consider when seeking to address any sort of trust issues, and that makes sense since if you do not trust yourself, you're never likely to trust someone else. If it comes to trust your loved one, you will have to have a critical look at yourself, and no, we aren't talking about believing in yourself. All you have to know when it comes to trust problems is that they often turn into an issue because you're struggling with some type of questions. For example, if you're concerned about your partner cheating on you, it might be associated with you having ideas about cheating them.

Trust-Building Exercises

Trust-building exercises may help to build it back again, but they may also be used to earn a fantastic and healthier relationship. If you're all set to focus on fixing these problems, below are a few very efficient exercises you should try.

Fall Back

Probably this is the most known one, as everyone has heard about it, but also the most difficult one to execute, even if you fully trust your partner. This exercise requires that you stand facing your spouse and just let yourself fall back, expecting them to grab you.

CHAPTER 6:

Touch Often

Touch was the first form of communication we understood as infants. Therefore, it can affect us in a much deeper way than mere words. As adults, we develop filters and defenses that help protect us from being affected by words. Nowadays, we are bombarded by so many advertisements that we learn to diminish the impact of almost everything we hear. Yet, touch is different. We tend to think that a person's touch is very "honest," whereas their words are subject to question. A loving touch can slide past a person's defenses and touch them at their core if you want to know how to powerfully and efficiently give your partner the three you need to learn how to touch your mate lovingly.

Loving touch is entirely different than a sexual touch. Some people confuse the two, and they end up paying a high price. Sexual touching is excellent, but it doesn't replace what a nonsexual touch can do. Many of my female clients complain that their partner never touches them unless they want to have sex. When this occurs, women typically interpret this behavior as the man saying, "I don't really like you, but I'm willing to have sex with you to satisfy my own selfish needs." It's no wonder that their partner's touch does not arouse women in such situations. Yet, when men frequently touch their partners in a caring, nonsexual manner, the women feel safe and loved. When a woman feels truly safe and loved, she becomes much more interested in sex than when she feels she is being used.

Men and women are different when it comes to their sexual and emotional needs. In a recent study, 70 percent of all women said they would gladly never have sexual intercourse again as long as they were able to cuddle or have a long hug each day with their partner. I advise my counseling clients to find out their partner's precise touching needs and satisfy them as best they can. Although there are a few exceptions, the basic rule in relationships is the more you satisfy your partner's needs, the more they will want to satisfy your needs. I encourage couples to communicate about the precise forms of touch them most and least desirable. We tend to assume that other people are like us, which just isn't true. As you and your partner regularly touch each other in enjoyable ways, the amount of intimacy in your relationship will skyrocket.

Laurie and Jeff came to my office, complaining of a lack of passion in their relationship. They were both successful career people, highly intelligent, and very friendly with each other. They even communicated pretty well and were adept at avoiding blame or arguments. Everything was in good working order from the neck up, but there was no energy from the neck down. They would have sex about twice a month, but it lacked passion. They came to me wondering what, if anything, was wrong. I asked them how much they touch each other throughout the day. They each gave me a look like, "What does that have to do with anything?" From the expressions on their faces, I knew I had hit pay dirt. Their minds were being massaged with friendly words and good conversation, but their hearts, bodies, and souls were being ignored.

They took the prescribed medicine. A week after, they were physically all over each other in our counseling session, whereas before, they had been on opposite sides of the couch. If I hadn't been there forcing them to be civilized, I think they would have made love right there in my office! Nonsexual touch regularly can be strong love medicine.

CHAPTER 7:

Create Shared Rituals

Exploration proposes that couples who are fun-loving together have closer and more fulfilling relationships.

Shockingly, we people will, in general, become less perky as we get more seasoned. Play requires a touch of opportunity and space; by definition, it is anything but a profitable action. Life schedules and worries can infringe on our relationship and drain the fun-loving nature out of it.

Why Is Trouble Being Fun-Loving?

Why are people fun-loving? That probably won't be a question you've at any point posed to yourself. However, it's one that consumes the psyches of developmental scholars, even though (at least on its surface) play doesn't appear to add to our endurance. As opposed to investing the time chasing for food or resting to set aside energy, why would it be valuable for our progenitors to stay nearby the fire doing amusing impersonations of one another? Wouldn't that divert them from potential dangers that may be crawling out of the shrubs?

Playfulness, a few scientists guess, could fill in as a sign to expected mates. Men who take part in a benevolent, corresponding play with others may be exhibiting their absence of hostility — an attractive characteristic when savage guys are a danger to their spouses and kids — and ladies who have the energy for play may be showing their energy, an intermediary for their conceptive capacities. At least that is how individual analysts decipher the finding that, as per studies, individuals appear to search for playfulness, humor, and a carefree demeanor in possible partners.

What Does romantic Play Resemble?

We can take numerous energetic ways toward intimacy — and there's something we can gain from how analysts have listed, sorted, and accounted for all the various ways partners play.

One of the most widely recognized types of play is by all accounts the mystery language that creates between couples, from monikers to private jokes.

The pretense is likewise standard. In the solace of the romantic bubble, one may have a sense of security enough to claim to be a little dog, make their best Elvis impression, or mirror the neighbor's strangely piercing snicker.

Some play requires no words by any means — my partner's moving being one model. We can energetically steal a treat from our cherished, transforming a typically childish act into a warm trade. Prodding is another behavior that pushes it among positive and negative, so play is a fragile exchange: Our partner needs to see our perky aim and participate in the game if they are irritated by our silliness put off by our come emotionally pokes.

Some play is more organized, similar to the guidelines and games that couples create. When I'm discussing Fred over a Google-able purpose of actuality, we frequently wager three kisses on the appropriate response before finding it

— and the washout needs to pay their obligation promptly.

In these manners, play appears to emerge precipitously. In any case, then those erratic remarks or practices transform into propensities, transforming and advancing after some time yet continually communicating a first love and comprehension.

In this way, it most likely shocks no one that lively couples are frequently cheerful couples. In considers that recall individuals about their practices and feelings, the individuals who are perkier in their relationships will, in general, experience increased positive emotions, be happier with their relationship, and feel closer to one another. They report that they convey better, resolve clashes better, and see their links positively.

What Sort of Play Will Work for You?

When we think about our relationships, those fun-loving minutes are things to esteem. In the ordinary, two individuals energetically develop a mystery language and culture in the ordinary's daily schedule, and it is exclusively their own. Play includes demonstrating our partner parts of ourselves that others once in a while observe, the uncorrupt, senseless side that probably won't be socially adequate at work or in different settings. Playing is inspecting the obscure outskirts of two minds, whose forms can turn out to be reassuringly natural just through the experience of shared weakness and nonjudgmental responsiveness. It is through playing that we figure out how to move toward somebody's more cozy self.

Consequently, there's nobody a size-fits-all approach to play with your partner. Each couple's play will look somewhat changed, and that is the point. If there were any solution, it would be something like this: Let your senseless self-come out, value the silliness of your cherished one, and do what makes you both grins.

CHAPTER 8:

Develop Active Listening

If you want to build healthy communication skills, listening is essential. It will only help you build a long-lasting, happy relationship. When you feel you are being heard, you feel empowered. It will give you a boost to share even more because other people will show they care.

They'll acknowledge what you say and validate you. You need to do the same to validate your partner. Listening must go both ways; there can't be only one side listening. This will make one of you feel unappreciated and will disconnect you. The relationship will suffer.

Before we learn how to listen, let's look at the reasons why we don't listen. It could be because of distractions or the inability to focus. We all experience these barriers, and we need to overcome them to learn active listening.

There are different types of blocks we encounter when we should be carefully listening. They are easy to overcome with some extra focus, but you won't notice if you don't become aware of them. So, let's list some.

1. **Comparing:** This usually happens when we listen to our partner talk, but we continuously compare his experience with our own. This block is familiar with people who have insecurities.

2. **Mind reading:** It happens when the one who listens tries to predict what the speaker will say after or tries to figure out what the speaker means or feels.

3. **Rehearsing:** This happens when the one who is supposed to be listening is obsessed with what he will respond to the speaker, or if he is following to talk.

4. **Filtering:** If we find a particular subject unpleasant, we can often catch our mind wandering and not be prepared to listen to the unpleasant story.

5. **Dreaming:** Simply put, the listener is daydreaming and not paying attention to the speaker.

6. **Identifying:** The listener often interrupts the speaker to share his experience with a particular subject.

7. **Advising:** The listener interrupts the speaker with the advice he or she has to offer even before the speaker is done with his story.

8. **Sparring:** This happens when the listener is interrupting the speaker to disagree or to debate.

9. **Being right:** This happens when the listener does not allow the speaker to prove him wrong.

10. **Derailing:** The listener, for one reason or another, changes the subject.

11. **Placating:** The listener is more focused on being supportive and sounding pleasant than listening.

We all have listening blocks, some of which we are aware of, and some aren't. Listening blocks are the bad habits that will hold our relationship back. We need to get rid of these bad habits if we want to build a healthy, long-lasting relationship. Which of the listening blocks listed above do you recognize in yourself? It can be more than one depending on the situation and the person who is speaking. Think of your partner. You probably know what in his tone triggers one of these listening blocks. For a happy relationship, it is of great importance to be open but not just about yourself. You also need to be open about the things your partner is telling you.

Learn active Listening

Now that you are aware of your listening blocks, you must engage the conversation process and listen to your partner. Active listening means you can respond to your partner's stories, not just with words but with body language and facial expressions.

This will not only tell your reactions; it will also indicate that you are genuinely listening.

As a person with relationship insecurities, there are things available for you to help you not just be a better listener but to learn more about your insecurities, and you will see them clearly for what they are:

- **Paraphrasing:** When dealing with insecurities, it is essential to paraphrase what your partner is saying. This will leave no space for miscommunication, and you will know what your partner is communicating. Paraphrasing is useful for remembering conversations, and if you bring it up, there will be no misunderstandings.

- **Clarifying:** It is more an extension of paraphrasing, but it means you will ask questions to make sure you understand your partner. You will get more information by doing so, and you will be able to fill any gaps you had in understanding. It will also let your partner know you are actively communicating with him or her.

- **Feedback:** Simply respond to your partner's story. You can even talk about how their story influenced you and how it made you feel. Giving feedback is an excellent opportunity to open up and be honest with your partner. But be sure to ask your partner how he feels about his story. You might have an understanding of his thoughts, but you are still uncertain of how he feels. Don't shy away from asking questions when you are giving feedback.

CHAPTER 9:

Manage Your Anger

Anger partly makes inroads into interpersonal relationships, and in specific ways and sizes that come in, we don't always identify as anger. There's the screaming, aggressive version that most of us think about when we hear someone get angry — the kind of anger that depletes. Some of us don't like being around people who are outwardly and aggressively angry, and some of us react in ways that are incredibly unhelpful and even detrimental to us.

And there is anger which doesn't feel like anger at all. Imagine I'm mad because you didn't turn up for a lunch date on time. Rather than calmly telling you how I feel (confused and irritated), I feel nothing is wrong. If you're trying to talk with me, I'm listening to you barely and minimally, making you make all the effort. Soon you would be able to say, "What's the matter?" I'm saying,

"What are you talking about? There's nothing wrong with that!" If not noisy and offensive, passive-aggression is dangerous in its unique way.

Understanding the Impact of Anger on Your Relationship

Do you live with a partner's wrath, which has become a constant source of discomfort to you? Do you now feel like your whole life is designed to stop, deter, or monitor your partner's anger? And do you think that your partner's anger is a vortex that pulls you in, drives you to join in the outrage, and contributes to an endless series of wars, combat battles, and scorekeeping? Many of the other couples follow each other's lead, and their routines seem unchanging.

Disharmonious speech by one partner sets the stage for the other. In these unacceptable displays of frustration, all these people have been lost; no one can clarify what needs to be said or settle problems that cook under the surface.

It's only standard that you become angry in reaction to what you believe is an unjust hostility directed towards you. It's only fair that your partner takes responsibility for changing the drill when it feels like your partner's anger is pulling the rug from under you. Exactly right?

How We Get Entangled

If you're in a well-established and loving relationship with this person, it makes sense to want them to be encouraged to make some changes. How do you keep the rush because your partner doesn't seem to have it?

What Options Do You Have?

If the relationship stays the way it is and you continue to live unhappily with this person, when is the time to say "enough?" Proposing to leave a committed relationship may be easy for someone else, particularly when children and other shared responsibilities tie you together, but it's never an easy option.

As we'll be addressing, setting firm boundaries on what's reasonable and what you're reluctant to consider is critical to deciding to leave. You will leave immediately if your safety or that of other family members is in jeopardy.

First, we're going to explore the real possibilities that you can, directly and indirectly, influence what's happening to this person after so you don't have to plan an escape.

To address these problems, you need to know more about the dynamics of the relationships: what you do will influence what the other person thinks and feels, and then decide to do so. The reverse is also real — what your partner immediately impacts on you and can set the stage for you to make changes you never thought you'd be making.

The Nature of Change in Relationships

How are you changing someone when that person hasn't wanted to do it on their own and can't even believe there's a problem there?

Let's look at what you can personally handle, and at the disadvantages of your strength. I'm not going to suggest that I can control any other living thing.

Seek to "make" a polite adolescent all the time, or a three-year-old live in the backyard, without building a fence, if you don't believe me. We'll be seeking help from others.

We will praise and thank them if they impress us, and even reject or punish them in some way if they fail to meet our expectations. And we limit ourselves to persuasion and feedback — not to control. And this also extends to the situations in which we love others to carry out their angry feelings.

There's one silver lining, though. And if we can't guilt-trip or threaten enough to get others to stop the bad things they're doing, we're mostly liable for what we're doing in response or proactively handling living with a wrathful person. When recalling what you are doing now when your loved one is unreasonably angry or lonely, you will also be determining how effective the solution has been and taking steps to strengthen it.

Learning a new Pattern

It's not easy to break free from a routine you're used to, even though you know you've been trapped. Psychologist Harriet Lerner describes the interdependent behaviors of a couple as a "dance." Each one has "steps" that impact on what the other is doing. Behavioral habits can get so unconscious that we engage in them without fully aware of what we're doing. So, in general, the first step is to become conscious, when upset, of exactly how we respond to a loved one's "dance movements." If you don't like the new "dance," the steps may shift, and your partner may or may not follow your lead-but the old "dance of rage" is over.

CHAPTER 10:

Reduce The Use of Social Media and digital Devices

Innovation is inevitable in the contemporary globe. A couple of work continues to be that they do not need a daily computer system; social media sites have linked people worldwide. The internet has also become the go-to resource of details. Facebook has, somehow, replaced the night news as people's means of learning more about worldwide and national events. Instagram and also YouTube have developed an entirely brand-new breed of celeb. In contrast, the easy availability of photo editing and enhancing software has permitted a generation of models to look impossibly remarkable on paper. The globe has become wired, and with the arrival of smart devices, and most individuals are linked to the digital earth from the moment they get up in the early morning.

Considerable innovation use has been linked to stress and anxiety, sleeplessness, anxiety, and depression. Also, a few of the electronic age's most positive attributes are the reason for these significant troubles. The web contains info in any way times, from practical realities about damaging news or identifying a cardiovascular disease to baffling triviality such as how many bananas a person would certainly have to consume to struggle with potassium poisoning and also warmed debates about the length of time it would undoubtedly consider zombies to overwhelm significant cities.

Living bordered by this deluge of information triggers information overload. The brain has a hard time sorting with the consistent flow of details, and also, a person starts to stay in a state of subconscious anxiety and stress. This is because the brain is hardwired to filter information, mainly aesthetic details such as the photos and text that make up most of the material on the internet. This uncontrollable and subconscious examination is a holdover transformative trait from when stopping working from evaluating aesthetic information appropriately could cause a person to get eaten by a starving lion.

The brain, nevertheless, is an astonishingly adaptable body organ. Eventually, it finds out to more or less stay on par with the constant flow of info. It discovers to expect the overwhelming influx of new data, and also being able to manufacture even more details is much better, right? Wrong. The mind sheds the capability to focus on something for an extended period because it is regularly expecting brand-new excitement. This is called "uniqueness addiction," or, more informally, "snacks brain." Smartphones only aggravate this neurological overstimulation since the web goes to a person's fingertips whatsoever times.

Heavy mobile phone usage can result in smartphone dependency, a subset of net addiction. Many individuals experience this condition that it has all but come to be the standard in society. Think of it, the number of people find it strange when a pal is twitchy throughout the day because they forgot their phone in your home? Do individuals act shocked if the pal's initial response to getting their phone back is to scroll hysterically via their texts, emails, as well as social media, feeds to see what they missed out on? The odd or impolite person is the one that tells their meant conversation partner to do away with their mobile phone until both are done speaking.

This obsession with smartphones likewise puts social media at an individual's fingertips, and also social networks itself is the source of numerous troubles. Possibly one of the most overlooked concerns with social media sites is the effect it has on rest. Hundreds of people keep up late during the night, scrolling through Facebook or switching breaks on Snapchat. This late-night social media scrolling results in countless people skipping out on slumber both due to bedtime and because the blue light from electronic screens reduces melatonin production. Such social media sites-based insomnia is an even more severe issue for teenagers that make up a substantial percentage of today's social media site users because teens need even more rest than adults.

Social media site likewise leads to stress and anxiety, envy, as well as clinical depression. People put their lives on social media sites and unconsciously obsess over how many likes their blog posts obtain. Considering that social media sites allow people to portray themselves as a particular method, most people only see the very best items of their Facebook good friends' lives. This leads to coveting, resentment, and also misery with their own life. Continuous contact with the online world likewise opens the doors for cyberbullying. This form of intimidation can be a lot more ferocious and destructive than in-person bullying since the bully can hide behind their keyboard's anonymity. There is no way, in most cases, for the sufferer to eliminate back. In acute situations, some teens have been cyberbullied so terribly that they have ended up being self-destructive.

Social media sites' adverse results on genuine relationships have brought about a generation of teens and kids that feel separated and lonesome. The social network does not just disrupt the right relations.

There is a large amount of excellent that can appear in technology, but it has a dark side that many people cheerfully disregard. Offered the rising prices of teen self-destruction and enhancing grievances about university graduates who cannot hold a typical discussion, it is time that individuals attend to the very genuine threats of the electronic age. They require to assess precisely how technology usage is connected to anxiety and choose what kind of interpersonal abilities they want their youngsters to have when they grow up. However, people need first to utilize their mind to do what it was indicated to do. They need to stop seeking to Lord Google and Woman iPhone for answers and also believe.

CHAPTER 11:

Learn to Love Yourself

Can you tell me frankly you love yourself? Have you had a hard time being comfortable with yourself? Focusing on your shortcomings is too simple that everyone will focus on their insecurities rather than on the things about themselves they're pleased with. Doing this will make you hate yourself. You can also be too distracted to concentrate on those around you and not concentrate on enjoying yourself. Some people don't want to be isolated, so they are afraid to do anything themselves. It will also delay your self-love path because you have to learn to be confident with yourself. So, keep reading and figure out how to treat one another today.

And, we'll take a look at specific ways you can fall in love with yourself and help you get going on your path towards self-esteem. Let's first remember that you deserve to respect yourself.

Why Is It So important to Love Yourself?

Some might think this more important than others, but self-love is one of the best things you can do for yourself.

Falling in love with yourself gives you faith, self-esteem, and can simply make you more optimistic. You may also note that falling in love is better for you because you have first learned to love yourself.

Facts about Self Love in Relationships

1. **People Treat You the Way They See You Treat Yourself**

   If you handle yourself with no respect or affection, you are effectively encouraging someone to do the same. Place yourself high expectations, then. Be willing to get up and say, "I am stronger than this. I won't tolerate that happening to me. "If you don't love yourself first, you won't have any standard of how others should treat you. It's much harder to understand that you have pure self-love that people give you less than you deserve.

2. **You Can't Depend on other People to Make You Feel Loved**

It can lead to dysfunctional relationships not only with others but with yourself, relying on other people to make you feel special.

If you don't have a romantic relationship with yourself, you will still not represent love in your relationships with others.

At least not in the way you could when you first knew yourself. It is the same idea as to when we're talking about self-care, "you can't drink from an empty cup." Visualize filling yourself with inside out passion. Unlike the outside in that will depend on other people to make you feel safe.

Fill yourself with so much passion that it is pouring out of your relationships with others.

3. **A Relationship Should Be a Relationship, Not a codependent Situation**

It comes back to the argument of not making you feel loved or deserving of relying on other men. Codependency is described as "excessive emotional or psychological reliance on a partner, usually a partner who needs help due to sickness or addiction." Typically, this dysfunctional relationship can grow if both spouses severely lose self-love, self-confidence, self-worth, etc. There are different rates of this, but it's not a safe condition, regardless.

4. **No One Can Make You happy the Way You Can Make Yourself happy**

That is real! I think who knows you better than you do? Learn how to make yourself happy to communicate how they can make you happy to future partners.

Anyway, if your relationship with yourself isn't yet there, you can end up ruining a perfectly good relationship. If you don't know how to be happy and just derive joy from your relationship, you place a lot of pressure on your partner to keep you happy always. Such pressure is unfair and can end up damaging the whole relationship.

How to Love Yourself?

Here are only 15 ideas that you should use and figure out how to enjoy yourself and get your confidence today!

1. **Have Fun by Yourself**

   It's always nice to schedule for yourself a couple of days, that's just for you to do something fun. You can learn to enjoy your own business by doing so, and most definitely become more comfortable about doing so on your own.

2. **Travel Once a Year**

   It may be out of the comfort zone altogether, but that is a positive thing! If you can fly alone, this would be an excellent taste of self-love. You're going to discover new things not only about yourself but also about a different world. It makes you get out of your daily schedule, too.

3. **Start a Journal**

   If you can write down your ideas and emotions, so any time, you can look out and see how you coped in those circumstances.

4. **Give Yourself a Break**

   We may often be harsh on ourselves, that's normal, but you have to allow yourself a break from time to time.

5. **Make a List of Your Accomplishments**

   Creating a list of what you've accomplished is a great way to fall in love. That makes you feel good about yourself, and from what you have accomplished, find happiness. Sometimes we can focus on the negatives and forget about the positives, so this is a great way to remember what you've achieved.

6. **Pursue new Interests**

   Trying something different that you wanted to do for a while or too afraid to do is perfect. Until you try it, you never know what you might enjoy, so think of a new hobby you could try, or go to a place you wanted to go to for some time.

7. **Give Yourself Credit Where Credit Is Due**

   Feast on your successes! Much as when you mention your successes, celebrating your milestones is nice too. Tell us what you did, share your stories, and be proud of what you did. Give yourself that credit that you deserve.

8. **Work on Your Self-Trust**

   A perfect way to display self-love is to have faith in yourself and your intuition. You will most likely know what's best for you, and self-confidence is a step toward self-love.

9. **Take Care of Yourself**

Perhaps this one is trivial, but taking care of yourself plays a huge role in learning how to love yourself when others do not. When you're looking after yourself, you'll be the best version of yourself. Look at our self-care suggestions to get you going.

CHAPTER 12:

Apologize More Often

One critical way to build trust, rekindle intimacy, and connect emotionally with your partner is to learn to apologize when you hurt them. In the long-life journey of love as a couple, there will be moments of arguments and broken promises, which will result in hurting each other's feelings. At such times, learning to say "sorry" can save your relationship. Learning to apologize to your partner is a crucial life and marriage skill. It is difficult to say sorry or apologizes to your partner, mostly if you belong to the class of individuals who view that as a sign of weakness.

When you understand what it means to you and your spouse, offering an apology becomes easier. Apologizing is one way to show that you are selfless and care for your partner's feelings. It shows that you are treating your partner the way you wish to be treated when you are hurt.

It is a simple way to admit your faults, and that you are willing to correct yourself and try to do better after. It is a way to own up your mistakes by acknowledging that you are an imperfect human being, and you can be wrong sometimes. It shows that you are willing to make an effort to grow from your mistakes and become a better partner.

Admit Your Mistakes

The first essential step in learning to apologize to your husband or wife is to admit that you are a human being and are eligible for making a mistake. This makes it easier for you to accept that you have a problem, and you are wrong in one way or another. Unless you accept that you are wrong, your apology cannot be genuine, sincere, or meaningful. You will just say it for the sake of avoiding a further argument, and it may not reflect your actual position, attitude, or facial expression.

So the first thing is learning to admit and accept your mistakes. Show that you are willing to be fully responsible for what you did and take the necessary corrective measures going forward.

Learn to Respect, the Emotions of Your Partner

When our partners do something wrong, we get hurt. Anyone who has been in a relationship knows this to be accurate, and it is a rule with no exceptions. All of us feel hurt when it happens. As you approach your partner for an apology, it is good to keep this in mind after doing something wrong. Show that it wasn't intentional and put yourself into your partner's shoes. This will show that you respect how they feel, and you will do your best to avoid making them feel the same after.

Be sincere with Your Apology

Listen to your partner as they vent out, and do not interfere until they have finished explaining how they feel. This will help you understand their perspective and the extent to which your actions have hurt them. That way, you will offer a sincere and honest apology reflecting your true feelings and attitude towards how they feel. Don't begin to explain why you did what you did or start to give excuses.

This will be a sign that you don't care, because you will be trying to justify your deeds. Be as specific as possible in your apology and just focus on that one issue at hand, which your partner has raised.

Humble Yourself and Ask for Forgiveness

It shows how humble and caring you are to your spouse when you present yourself in person and offer a face-to-face apology. You may want to write a letter, send an email, or a text message, but that should come as a way to emphasize what you have already verbalized. If you find it hard to face your spouse and verbalize the apology, you need to dig deep and unearth what prevents you from doing the same.

Don't be that kind of a spouse who gathers the courage to communicate face to face only when fighting.

Master the courage to face your partner and offer an apology. After making an apology, take it one step further and ask your spouse to forgive you.

Forgive Yourself

To show compassion to your partner, you must be able to be compassionate with yourself first. To welcome and accept your partner's forgiveness, you must be ready to forgive yourself too. It may not be easy to forgive yourself, especially after realizing the severity of the extent of the emotional damage you have caused your partner. Forgiving yourself gives you the confidence to work on yourself and make critical changes to rise above your mistakes. Failure to forgive yourself can make you begin to play the victim. You may end up with inward resentment, which can make it hard for you to forgive or accept forgiveness from your spouse. This can limit your chances of becoming better.

Create an Action Plan

You don't want to keep on apologizing all the time for doing the same things. The best way to avoid the same issues from cropping up is to develop an action plan. You need to develop a list of things or steps you will follow to avoid repeating mistakes. It makes no sense to your partner when you keep repeating mistakes and apologizing every time you do so. If it was a communication mishap, focus on improving your communication skills. If it was a delayed payment of some bills, come up with a way to remind yourself of such responsibilities. You can set a reminder on your phone or the calendar.

Put Your Action Plan into Practice

Take bold steps to practice your action plan. No amount of rhetoric can take the place of what you do. As they say, action speaks louder than words. Let your actions reflect your commitment to making sure that the same issues don't arise again by acting your words. Change your behavior by putting the requisite effort to make up for your faults. This will eliminate any fears or doubts your spouse might have developed as a result of your mistakes. They will begin to rebuild their trust and intimacy once they see that you are putting a lot of effort into becoming better.

CHAPTER 13:

Spice Up Your Sex Life

Why does good sex fade even when couples love each other very much? Can we want what we already have? Why is forbidden so erotic? What is it about indiscretion that makes desire so potent?

And why does sex make babies, but babies make way for erotic train-smashes between couples? When you love, how does it feel? And when you desire, how is that different? These are some of the questions that we face in modern love.

Talking about modern love, let's just refer back to how our modern (millennial) society is becoming increasingly individualistic. A big part of our relationships entails sex and sexual desires, so we need to look at how we approach it today and age.

Today, we still need to feel secure. We want predictability, dependability, reliability. We need anchoring experiences in our lives. A place to call home. But, in the same breath, we also don't want to feel stuck in a mundane routine. We have a kind of contradicting need, too — and it's an intense need. It is a need for adventure, novelty, mystery, risk, danger, the unexpected and mysterious. We want to travel and see things, but we also want a place to call home.

These kinds of options weren't readily available to most couples or marriages back in the day. Marriage used to be more of an economic institution in which people were given a partnership for life for social status, children, and companionship. Today, however, we still seek these "perks"— but besides, we want our partners to be our best friends, confidants, economic partners, and insatiable lovers. And on top of that, we live twice as long, so these wants and needs have to be maintained over a much more extended period.

We are expecting one person to give us what a whole community used to provide. We ask for belonging, identity, consistency, but also transcendence and mystery.

We ask for comfort and edge. We ask for novelty and familiarity. We ask for predictability and surprise. No wonder we're so confused when it comes to relationships and sex. We are sitting with a crisis of desire.

Yet our crisis of desire is in our minds. And again, it all comes down to a mindful approach to our relationship. Even when it comes to sex, no, wait, especially when it comes to sex.

Once we are aware that we are facing a crisis of desire, and that the crisis nestled itself into our minds and imaginations, we can do something about it.

Keep this in mind when you go into the bedroom. It doesn't matter if you're in a committed relationship and want to spice things up or if you're just starting out and still getting to know each other.

Take a mindful moment to remind yourself (and even your partner) that your imagination lies at the heart of keeping the spark of desire ignited. Now, let's allow our imaginations to run wild for a while with some of the ideas below!

Dirty Weekend Getaway

I know we said mystery is not a place to go but instead looking through new eyes. Still, it doesn't mean that we have to completely discard the mystery and adventure you can experience by visiting a new destination. Some alone time away in an unknown place elevates the sexiness factor.

Plus, if you reserve smartly, you don't even have to make the bed. Make a point to get jiggy at least once a day while you're away.

Play a Game

If playfulness is also one of the ingredients of "erotic intelligence," why not get into actually playing a game (or two). You could invest in some board games for couples, or just get the engines running with a round of strip poker. Or, set a timer so you can take turns choosing what to do after. If need be, invest in a set of sex dice to get you going. Play around with your partner to see what games work for you both.

Talk about Your Fantasies

Perhaps you have always wanted to do it in a pool. Maybe he wanted to do it on the beach. Or maybe one of you has been curious about a little role play. It's time to get the image inside your head out on the sheets for your partner to explore with you. If you can't play them out, you can always pretend. If you can't do it on the Great Wall of China, try acting like the long corner couch is the wall. This can go hand in hand with "playing games" or just keeping that playful, creative spirit alive.

Switch Things Up

Don't just always stick to the trusty old' featherbed. There are so many locations in the house, or even just within your room. You can try some new music or do it at a different time of the day. Keeping things as fresh and new as possible is vital. And then, of course, there are so many resources and ideas for some new positions that it might be great fun to search online where you and your partner can work through!

New Lingerie

New lingerie might not be the most mindful thing. Women underestimate the level of confidence some fancy lingerie can bring to the table. You can even take your partner along on the shopping trip. Men are visual creatures, and the anticipation will make them feel randy up until the grand reveal. Alternatively, just grab a few new items you feel confident in and surprise him when he gets home.

Be a little naughty

Get out of your comfort zone by trying a little dirty talk. Perhaps try a little spanking or make your partner wear a blindfold. Bring in a little tickle feather. Keep it playfully naughty.

Double the Foreplay

This one is for pleasing the ladies. Though men are visual creatures and go nuts in anticipation of some sexy time, women may need some more revving up. Touch her all over. Be gentle yet firm. Oh, and boys? Be thorough. Let her linger — she will make it clear when she has reached her limit.

Daytime Flirting!

Remember, folks, the whole game of sex is our imagination and our anticipation regarding our desires.

Why wait to flirt only in the bedroom?

If you want to spice things up, make an effort to flirt with each other all day long.

Shush the Bedroom Ambiance

Do away with a cluttered bedroom and make way for some candles.

Use the silk sheets now and then.

Warm up the room.

Add some soft music.

The more inviting the room, the sooner you'll be nestled in each other's arms… to say the least.

Add Sex Slots to the Calendar

It may seem boring to plan sex at first glance, but it can bring sex to a new level! Both partners have some time for grooming, buying a sexy outfit — whatever turns you two on. And don't just choose a date and time. Choose a place, a game you're going to play, a new position to try, and more.

CHAPTER 14:

Practice Empathy

Now that you understand a little more about empathy, you have to start communicating with it in mind. If you struggle with finding the right things to say, the following statements might help you figure it out.

Acknowledge Your Partner's Pain

You need to acknowledge how they feel at all times. They will feel supported when you connect with their struggle or pain.

You may use the following sentences:

- "I am sorry that you have to go through this."
- "I hate that this happened to you."
- "I wish I could turn things around and make it easier for you."

- "This must be hard for you."
- "I can see that this must be a difficult situation for you."

Share Your Feelings

You can be truthful and admit it when you don't know what to say or do. It is not always easy to imagine what the other person is going through. Share your thoughts and let your partner know that you are trying. You may use the following sentences:

- "I wish I could make things better."
- "My heart hurts for you."
- "I can't imagine how hard this must be for you."
- "I'm unfortunate that this happened to you."
- "I'm sorry that you are feeling this way."

Show Your Partner that You Are Grateful When They Open Up to You

People find it challenging to open up and be vulnerable to others. More often than not, their trust has been broken at some point. So, when they choose to trust you, you need to be grateful and express it. Show your partner you appreciate that they share their thoughts and emotions with you. Acknowledge how difficult it can be for them to do this sometimes.

You may use the following sentences:

- "I'm glad that you shared this with me."
- "I'm glad that you are telling me this."
- "I can imagine how hard it must be to talk about this. Thank you for sharing it with me."
- "I appreciate you trying to work hard on our relationship. I know you are trying, and that gives me hope."
- "Thank you for trusting me and opening up. I want to be there for you."

Show Your Partner that You Are Interested.

You have to take an interest in what your partner is going through. It can be hard to go through difficult times alone. You have to reach out and show them that you are there for support. Show them that you are interested in listening to whatever they have to say. Don't offer too much advice or too many opinions. Just be a good listener.

You may use the following sentences:

- "I'm here for you if you want to talk."
- "How are you feeling about all that's been going on lately?"
- "Are you OK? Is there something you want to talk about?"
- "I think you're feeling like ____. Am I right? Did I misunderstand?"
- "What has this been like for you?"

Show Encouragement

When your loved one is going through a tough time, you have to be encouraging. But you need to go about this the right way. Don't try to fix their problem or offer unsolicited advice. Just encourage them in a way that makes them feel better and motivated. Show them that you care and that you believe in them.

You may use the following sentences:

- "You are strong, and I believe you can get through this."
- "I am always on your side. You should never feel alone."
- "I'm proud of everything that you have done."
- "You matter, and you should never question it."
- "You are a very talented person."

Show Support

Actions matter more than words at times. You can take some simple actions to show your partner you support and help them through tough times. You can send them flowers to make them feel better. You can do some chores for them. Just do anything that you feel they will appreciate, making their lives a little easier.

You may use the following sentences:

- "I want to do this for you."
- "I am always here to listen."
- "Is there anything I can do for you right now?"

- "Is there any way I can help?"
- "Tell me what you need."

But in the end, there is no fixed script when it comes to sympathy. You have to be more attuned to your partner's needs and act likewise. Half the work is just listening and being there for them. I hope the examples given here help you deal with such situations better and more empathetic.

Conclusion

Now, all that is left to do is get working on your relationship to ensure that it is as healthy as you would like it to be. Remember, the mindful relationship is one in which both parties can engage mindfully to recall what matters to them at the moment. It is one that will allow both parties to work together to focus on communicating honestly, calmly, and without judgment.

Mindfulness is the simple human capacity to be completely aware, know where we are and what we are doing, and not be too reactive or distracted by what's going on around us. It's not a woo-woo that you have to spend hours studying or flying to a distant land to discover. It's open to you and your partner right now.

The mindful relationship is one that will help you and your partner become the best couple you can be. It will help you to unlock your untapped potential. It will help you to figure out how to better process events that happen when they are stressed, or it can help you figure out how to solve conflicts.

Remember to make use of the varying activities designed to allow you and your partner to work together, or alongside each other, to allow you to be continuously dedicated and contribute to the betterment of your relationship. Over time, you will find that your bonds will strengthen. You will find that intimacy and love will burn brighter. Your relationship does not have to be perfect, but it should provide everything you are looking for if you and your partner are both committed to communicating fairly and respectfully

We are approached to tune in, be persistent, and comprehend our musings, propensities, and inclinations, so we may discover empathy for the pieces of ourselves that we dislike to such an extent. Dejection, outrage, dread, envy — they will, in general, exist in each one of us. Some have a hold on it; a few of us don't. Having a critical relationship relies upon our capacity to be distant from everyone else and with us. An insightful individual perceives that they are 'stick' to their accomplice out of a feeling of need.

Whether you have decided to begin implementing the activities or just work with the material provided for now, you will find that you are at a great advantage having access to insight to make your relationship better.

Remember to pay attention to the most common relationship conflicts that are out there. Ensure that you are not actively falling into the relationship, bad habits, or toxic tendencies mentioned. Keep in mind that you should put most of your focus on how to build up and nurture your relationship so that you know that it will be as useful and beneficial to you and your partner as possible. Relationships should be treated as a team with mindful respect toward each other as teammates. If you can do that, you and your partner will be able to take on the world. Good luck as you set out on your journey to bettering yourself. You and your partner can do it!

Made in the USA
Las Vegas, NV
06 December 2020

12215448R00059